Published by Creative Education
P.O. Box 227
Mankato, Minnesota 56002
Creative Education is an imprint of The Creative Company

Design by Stephanie Blumenthal

Photographs by by Getty (Ernst Haas/Hulton Archive; Hulton Archive/Staff;
Johner; Kean Collection/Staff; Kean Collection/Staff; Kean Collection/Staff;
Mary Evans Picture Library; Roger Viollet Collection; Travelpix Ltd;
ELIOT ELISOFON; Ed Freeman; Kenneth Garrett; Kenneth Garrett;
Sylvian Grandadam; Sylvian Grandadam; Sylvian Grandadam; Robert Harding;
Frans Lemmens; Ian Mckinnell; Richard Nowitz; Gerard Rollando; Stephen Studd)

Library of Congress Cataloging-in-Publication Data

Bodden, Valerie.
Pyramids / by Valerie Bodden.
p. cm. — (Built to last)
Includes index.
ISBN 978-1-58341-563-4
1. Pyramids—Egypt—Juvenile literature. I. Title. II. Series.

DT63.B55 2008
932—dc22   2006101035

First edition
2 4 6 8 9 7 5 3 1

PYRAMIDS | VALERIE BODDEN

CREATIVE EDUCATION

A worker stood under the hot sun in the country of Egypt. He looked at the other workers. He watched them push a big rock. They placed it on a huge building. The worker was proud to be helping to build this pyramid (*PEER-uh-mid*).

The pyramids are in the desert

THE PYRAMIDS ARE THE OLDEST STONE BUILDINGS IN THE WORLD. THEY ARE MORE THAN 4,500 YEARS OLD!

SOME PYRAMIDS LOOK LIKE
THEY HAVE STEPS GOING UP
THE SIDES. OTHER PYRAMIDS
HAVE SMOOTH SIDES.

Some pyramids have big steps

A pyramid is a tall building. It has four sides. The sides are shaped like triangles. They meet at a point at the top.

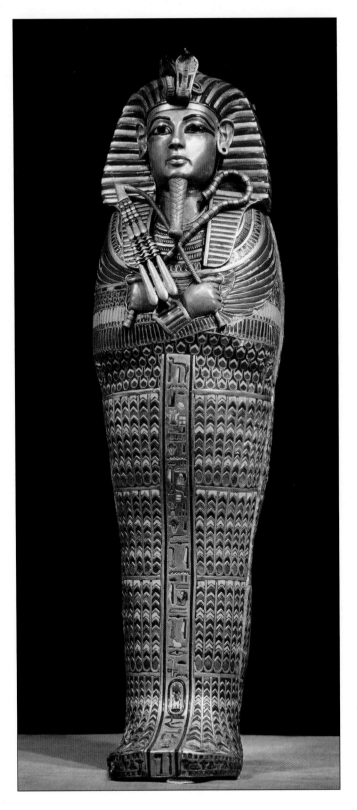

The pyramids of Egypt were built as tombs for Egypt's kings. The kings were called pharaohs (*FARE-ohs*). The people of Egypt built more than 90 pyramids.

Pharaohs were powerful kings

It took a lot of people to build a pyramid.
Some people think 80,000 men might
have worked on the pyramids! It took a
long time to build a pyramid, too. Most
pyramids took more than 20 years to build!

Lots of people go to see pyramids

THE BIGGEST PYRAMID IS CALLED THE GREAT PYRAMID. IT IS MADE OF ENOUGH STONE TO BUILD A LOW WALL ALL THE WAY AROUND EARTH!

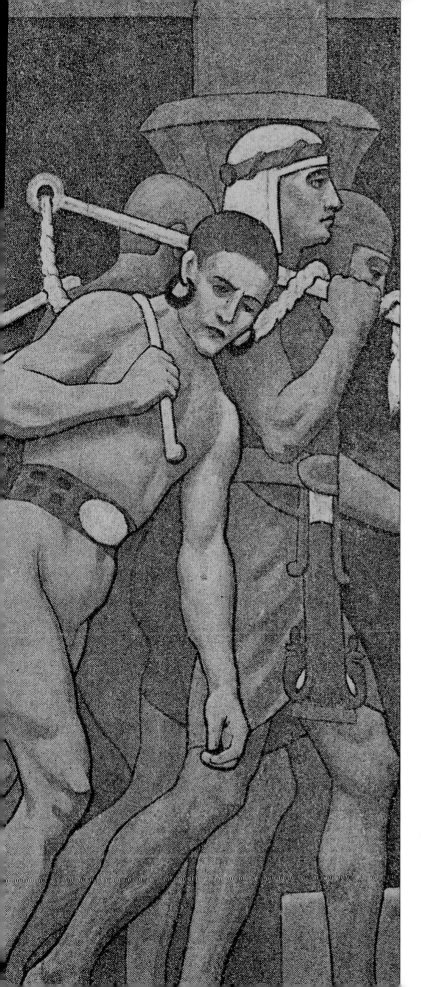

First, workers cut huge pieces of rock out of the ground. Then they dragged the rocks to a river. The rocks were put on a boat. The boats floated to where the pyramid was being built.

Dragging rocks was hard work

There, workers put the rocks in place.
To get up high, workers built a dirt ramp
next to the pyramid. They dragged the
rocks up the ramp.

AT THE TIME THE PYRAMIDS
WERE BUILT, THE PEOPLE OF
EGYPT WROTE WITH
PICTURES. THE PICTURES WERE
CALLED HIEROGLYPHS (*HY-
RUH-GLIFS*).

Hieroglyphs have animal pictures

When all the rocks were in place, workers put the capstone on top. Then they covered the pyramid with special white rocks. They rubbed the rocks until they were smooth. The rocks shone in the sun.

Pyramids look like mountains

Inside, a pyramid had a big room. This is where the pharaoh's body was put when he died. Some pyramids had a few small rooms, too. These rooms might have held things like treasure for the pharaoh to use in the afterlife.

BEFORE THE PHARAOHS WERE
PUT IN THE PYRAMIDS, THEY
WERE MADE INTO MUMMIES.
THEIR BODIES WERE
WRAPPED IN WHITE CLOTH.

Pyramids had mummies inside

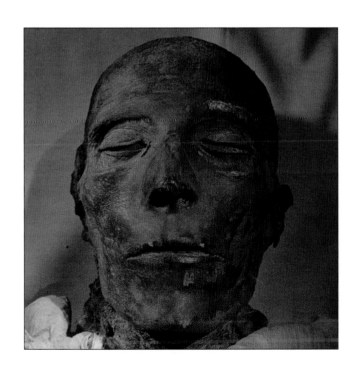

Today, many pyramids still stand. Some of them are falling apart. But people can go inside some pyramids. Then they can imagine what life was like when the pharaohs ruled Egypt!

Some pyramids had fancy art

ALL OF THE PYRAMIDS OF EGYPT WERE BROKEN INTO BY THIEVES (*THEEVZ*). THE THIEVES TOOK A LOT OF THE TREASURES INSIDE THE PYRAMIDS.